MAR 19 2007

Alexander Graham Bell
A LIFE OF HELPFULNESS

by Sheila Rivera

Lerner Publications Company • Minneapolis

Photo Acknowledgments

The photographs in this book appear with the permission of: The Granger Collection, New York, front cover, p. 22; © Stockbyte, p. 4; Library of Congress, pp. 6 (LC-G9-Z10-35), 8 (LC-G9-Z1-155, 874-A-2), 9 (LC-USZ62-104427), 12 (LC-USZ62-123312), 13 (LC-G9-Z1-14,503-A-1), 14 (LC-USZ62-115826), 18 (LC-USZ62-56429), 20 (LC-USZ62-134586), 25, 26; © Digital Vision/Getty Images, p. 10; © Bettmann/CORBIS, p. 15; © CORBIS, p. 16; © North Wind Picture Archives, p. 17; The Art Archive/Culver Pictures, p. 21; Courtesy The National Library of Medicine, p. 24.

Lerner Publications Company
A division of Lerner Publishing Group
241 First Avenue North
Minneapolis, MN 55401 U.S.A.

Website address: www.lernerbooks.com

Words in **bold type** are explained in a glossary on page 31.

Library of Congress Cataloging-in-Publication Data

Rivera, Sheila, 1970–
      Alexander Graham Bell : a life of helpfulness / by Sheila Rivera.
          p.   cm. – (Pull ahead books)
      Includes index.
      ISBN-13: 978-0-8225-6463–8 (lib. bdg. : alk. paper)
      ISBN-10: 0-8225-6463–7 (lib. bdg. : alk. paper)
      1. Bell, Alexander Graham, 1847–1922–Juvenile literature. 2. Inventors–United States–Biography–Juvenile literature. 3. Telephone–United States–History–Juvenile literature. I. Title.
TK6143.B4R58 2007
621.385092–dc22 [B]   2006021944

Manufactured in the United States of America
1 2 3 4 5 6 – JR – 12 11 10 09 08 07

Table of Contents

Talk to Me 5

A Helpful Father 7

In His Father's Footsteps 11

Helping the President 19

Helping Others 23

A Life of Helpfulness 27

Alexander Graham Bell
Timeline 28

More about
Alexander Graham Bell 30

Websites 30

Glossary 31

Index 32

Talk to Me

Ring, ring, ring! What's that sound? That's a telephone ringing. The telephone was created by Alexander Graham Bell, one of the world's greatest **inventors.** Alexander liked creating things that could help people.

Alexander *(right)* with *(from left)* his brother Melville, his father, his brother Edward, and his mother

A Helpful Father

Alexander Graham Bell was born in 1847. Alexander's mother was hard of hearing. His father was a speech teacher.

Alexander's father

Alexander's father liked to help others.
He taught people how to speak clearly.

He used pictures to show them how to make certain sounds.

[Pronounce the Nos.] [Names.]	[Name the Objects.]		[Name the Objects.]	
1.				
2.				
3				
4.				
5.				
6.				
7.				
8.				

[EXERCISE.]

One by one.
Two or three.
Four at once.
Five o'clock.
Half-past six.
Seven-thirty.
Eight to nine.
Ten or twelve.
Twice two, four.
Twice three, six.
Four and four, eight.
Nine and two, eleven.
Twice or thrice.

Two, a couple.
Twelve, a dozen.
Twenty, a score.
A book-case.
A few books.
New book-shelves.
A silver watch.
A gold watch.
The watch-key.
A good saw.
Cap and feather.
Tongs and shovel.
Sugar-tongs.

A hunting whip.
A table lamp.
A bunch of onions.
Corns and bunions.
A ship's boat.
A sailing boat.
Cart and horse.
A round tent.
Rows of houses.
A dog-kennel.
A little monkey.
A pretty cage.
A green canary.

This man holds cleaned wheat. Alexander made a machine that cleaned wheat quickly.

In His Father's Footsteps

Like his father, Alexander also liked to help others. Alexander made his first **invention** when he was still a boy. It was a machine that cleaned wheat.

This woman cleans wheat by pouring it onto the ground. As it falls, the wind blows away the unwanted part of the wheat.

People had to clean wheat before they could use it. It took a long time for them to clean it.

Alexander wanted to help. He made
a machine that cleaned a lot of
wheat quickly.

Alexander was a boy when he made his machine to clean wheat.

Alexander felt good when he helped others. Like his father, he became a teacher.

Alexander at age eighteen

Alexander taught **deaf** children how to speak.

Alexander shows a girl how to feel her throat move when she speaks.

Alexander and a worker test an invention.

Alexander also did lots of **experiments** with sound. He figured out how to send a voice over a wire.

This invention became known as the telephone.

Alexander talks into the first long-distance telephone.

James Garfield was the president in 1881.

Helping the President

In 1881, someone shot the president. Doctors could not find the bullet in his body. Alexander wanted to help. He made a machine that could locate metal in a person's body.

It took a few days for Alexander to complete his invention.

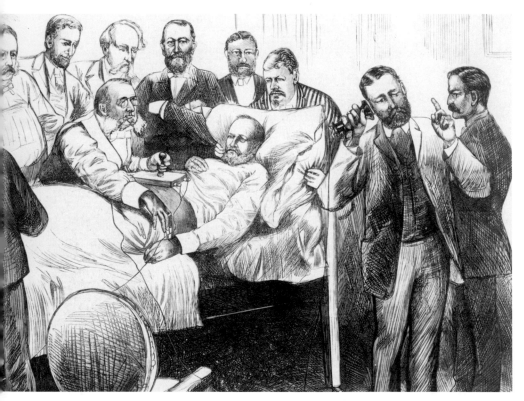

Alexander tries to find the bullet in President Garfield's body using his new machine.

But the president was too sick.
Alexander's invention could not save him.

Soldiers guard President Garfield's body before he is buried.

Alexander and his wife, Mabel

Helping Others

That same year, Alexander's wife, Mabel, had a baby. The couple named him Edward. The baby was born too early, and he could not **breathe** well. The baby died. Alexander was heartbroken.

A doctor checks a man who is having trouble breathing.

Alexander did not want other people to die because they could not breathe.

He wanted to help. He made a machine
that would help people breathe.

Alexander made this drawing of his breathing machine.

A Life of Helpfulness

With Alexander Graham Bell's telephone, people could talk to one another over long distances. His other inventions helped sick people get well. His work as a teacher helped deaf people communicate. His helpfulness made life better for many people.

ALEXANDER GRAHAM BELL TIMELINE

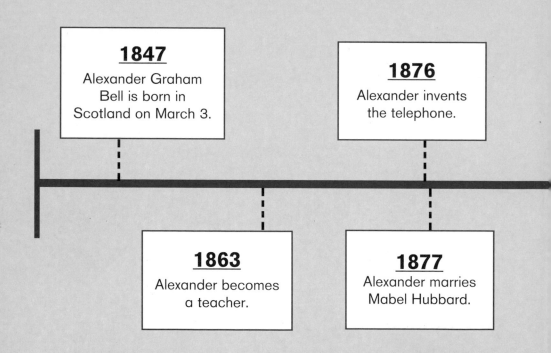

1847
Alexander Graham Bell is born in Scotland on March 3.

1876
Alexander invents the telephone.

1863
Alexander becomes a teacher.

1877
Alexander marries Mabel Hubbard.

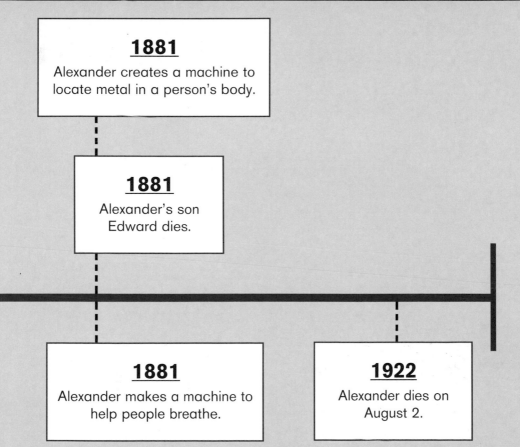

1881
Alexander creates a machine to locate metal in a person's body.

1881
Alexander's son Edward dies.

1881
Alexander makes a machine to help people breathe.

1922
Alexander dies on August 2.

More about Alexander Graham Bell

● Alexander Graham Bell was friends with Helen Keller. He introduced her to her teacher, Anne Sullivan.

● Alexander took more pride in his work with deaf people than in his invention of the telephone.

● Alexander's experiments included building boats and airplanes and taking salt out of saltwater.

Websites

Alexander Graham Bell
http://www.alexandergrahambell.org/

The Alexander Graham Bell Family Papers
http://memory.loc.gov/ammem/bellhtml/bellhome.html

Inventors—The History of the Telephone
http://inventors.about.com/library/inventors/
bltelephone.htm

Glossary

breathe: to take air into the lungs and force it out

deaf: unable to hear

experiments: tests done to find out or prove something

invention: an original creation

inventors: people who create new things

Index

Bell, Edward, 23, 29
Bell, Mabel, 23, 28
birth, 7, 28
breathing machine, 25, 29

experiments, 16, 30

family, 6–8, 22–23
father, 8

Garfield, James, 18–21

inventions, 5, 11, 13, 17, 19–21, 25, 27, 28–29, 30

Keller, Helen, 30

Sullivan, Anne, 30

telephone, 5, 17, 27, 28, 30

wheat-cleaning machine, 11, 13
work as a teacher, 14–15, 27, 28